'CIVILIZED' SEXUAL MORALITY AND MODERN NERVOUS ILLNESS

BY

SIGMUND FREUD

British Library Cataloguing-in-Publication Data
A catalogue record for this book is available from the
British Library

Contents

Sigmund Freud

Sigismund Schlomo Freud was born on 6th May 1856, in the Moravian town of Příbor, now part of the Czech Republic.

Sigmund was the eldest of eight children to Jewish Galician parents, Jacob and Amalia Freud. After Freud's father lost his business as a result of the Panic of 1857, the family were forced to move to Leipzig and then Vienna to avoid poverty. It was in Vienna that the nine-year-old Sigmund enrolled at the Leopoldstädter Kommunal-Realgymnasium before beginning his medical training at the University of Vienna in 1873, at the age of just 17. He studied a variety of subjects, including philosophy, physiology, and zoology, graduating with an MD in 1881.

The following year, Freud began his medical career in Theodor Meynert's psychiatric clinic at the Vienna General Hospital. He worked there until 1886 when he set up in private practice and began specialising in "nervous disorders". In the same year he married Merth Bernays, with whom he had 6 children between 1887 and 1895.

In the period between 1896 and 1901, Freud isolated himself from his colleagues and began work on developing the basics of his psychoanalytic theory. He published *The Interpretation of Dreams*, in 1899, to a lacklustre reception, but continued to produce works such as *The Psychopathology of Everyday Life* (1901) and *Three Essays on the Theory of Sexuality* (1905). He held a weekly meeting at his home known as the "Wednesday Psychological Society" which eventually developed into the Vienna Psycho-Analytic Society. His ideas gained momentum and by the end of the decade his methods were being used internationally by neurologists and psychiatrists.

Freud made a huge and lasting contribution to the field of psychology with many of his methods still being used in modern psychoanalysis. He inspired much discussion on the wealth of theories he produced and the reactions to his works began a century of great psychological investigation.

In 1930 Freud fled Vienna due to rise of Nazism and resided in England until his death from mouth cancer on 23rd September 1939.

'CIVILIZED' SEXUAL MORALITY AND MODERN NERVOUS ILLNESS
(1908)

In his recently published book, *Sexual Ethics*, Von Ehrenfels (1907) dwells on the difference between 'natural' and 'civilized' sexual morality. By natural sexual morality we are to understand, according to him, a sexual morality under whose dominance a human stock is able to remain in lasting possession of health and efficiency, while civilized sexual morality is a sexual morality obedience to which, on the other hand, spurs men on to intense and productive cultural activity. This contrast, he thinks, is best illustrated by comparing the innate character of a people with their cultural attainments. I may refer the reader to Von Ehrenfels's own work for a more extensive consideration of this significant line of thought, and I shall extract from it here only as much as I need as a starting-point for my own contribution to the subject.

It is not difficult to suppose that under the domination of a civilized sexual morality the health and efficiency of single individuals may be liable to impairment and that ultimately this injury to them, caused by the sacrifices imposed on them, may reach such a pitch that, by this indirect path, the cultural aim in view will be endangered as well. And

3

Von Ehrenfels does in fact attribute a number of ill-effects to the sexual morality which dominates our Western society to-day, ill-effects for which he is obliged to make that morality responsible; and, although he fully acknowledges its high aptitude for the furtherance of civilization, he is led to convict it of standing in need of reform. In his view, what is characteristic of the civilized sexual morality that dominates us is that the demands made on women are carried over to the sexual life of men and that all sexual intercourse is prohibited except in monogamous marriage. Nevertheless, consideration of the natural difference between the sexes makes it necessary to visit men's lapses with less severity and thus in fact to admit a *double* morality for them. But a society which accepts this double morality cannot carry 'the love of truth, honesty and humanity' (Von Ehrenfels, ibid. 32 ff.) beyond a definite and narrow limit, and is bound to induce in its members concealment of the truth, false optimism, self-deception and deception of others. And civilized sexual morality has still worse effects, for, by glorifying monogamy, it cripples the factor of *selection by virility* - the factor whose influence alone can bring about an improvement of the individual's innate constitution, since in civilized peoples *selection by vitality* has been reduced to a minimum by humanity and hygiene (ibid., 35).

Among the damaging effects which are here laid at the door of civilized sexual morality, the physician will miss a particular one whose significance will be discussed in detail in the present paper. I refer to the increase traceable to it of modern nervous illness - of the nervous illness, that is, which is rapidly spreading in our present-day society. Occasionally a nervous patient will himself draw the doctor's attention to the part played in the causation of his complaint by the opposition between his constitution and the demands of civilization and will say: 'In our family we've all become neurotic because we wanted to be something better than what, with our origin, we are capable of being.' Often, too, the physician finds food for thought in observing that those who succumb to nervous illness are precisely the offspring of fathers who, having been born of rough but vigorous families, living in simple, healthy, country conditions, had successfully established themselves in the metropolis, and in a short space of time had brought their children to a high level of culture. But, above all, nerve specialists themselves have loudly, proclaimed the connection between 'increasing nervous illness' and modern civilized life. The grounds to which they attribute this connection will be shown by a few extracts from statements that have been made by some eminent observers.

W. Erb (1893): 'The original question, then, is whether the causes of nervous illness that have been put before you are present in modern life to such a heightened degree as to account for a marked increase in that form of illness.

The question can be answered without hesitation in the affirmative, as a cursory glance at our present-day existence and its features will show.

'This is already clearly demonstrated by a number of general facts. The extraordinary achievements of modern times, the discoveries and inventions in every sphere, the maintenance of progress in the face of increasing competition - these things have only been gained, and can only be held, by great mental effort. The demands made on the efficiency of the individual in the struggle for existence have greatly increased and it is only by putting out all his mental powers that he can meet them. At the same time, the individual's needs and his demands for the enjoyments of life have increased in all classes; unprecedented luxury has spread to strata of the population who were formerly quite untouched by it; irreligion, discontent and covetousness have grown up in wide social spheres. The immense extension of communications which has been brought about by the network of telegraphs and telephones that encircle the world has completely altered the conditions of trade and commerce. All is hurry and agitation; night is used for travel, day for business, even 'holiday trips' have become a strain on the nervous system. Important political, industrial and financial crises carry excitement into far wider circles of people than they used to do; political life is engaged in quite generally; political, religious and social struggles, party-politics, electioneering, and the enormous spread of trade-unionism inflame tempers, place an ever greater strain on the mind, and encroach upon the hours for recreation, sleep and rest. City life is constantly becoming more sophisticated and more restless. The exhausted nerves seek recuperation in increased stimulation and in highly-spiced pleasures, only to become more exhausted than before. Modern literature is predominantly concerned with the most questionable problems which stir up all the passions, and which encourage sensuality and a craving for pleasure, and contempt for every fundamental ethical principle and every ideal. It brings before the reader's mind pathological figures and problems concerned with psychopathic sexuality, and revolutionary and other subjects. Our ears are excited and overstimulated by large doses of noisy and insistent music. The theatres captivate all our senses with their exciting performances. The plastic arts, too, turn by preference to what is repellent, ugly and suggestive, and do not hesitate to set before our eyes with revolting fidelity the most horrible sights that reality has to offer.

'This general description is already enough to indicate a number of dangers presented by the evolution of our modern civilization. Let me now fill in the picture with a few details.'

Binswanger (1896): 'Neurasthenia in particular has been described as an essentially modern disorder, and Beard, to whom we are indebted for a first comprehensive account of it believed that he had discovered a new nervous disease which had developed specifically on American soil. This supposition was of course a mistaken one; nevertheless, the fact that it was an *American* physician who was first able to grasp and describe the peculiar features of this illness, as the fruit of a wide experience, indicates, no doubt, the close connections which exist between it and modern life, with its unbridled pursuit of money and possessions, and its immense advances in the field of technology which have rendered illusory every obstacle, whether temporal or spatial, to our means of intercommunication.'

Von Krafft-Ebing (1895): 'The mode of life of countless civilized people exhibits nowadays an abundance of anti-hygienic factors which make it easy to understand the fateful increase of nervous illness; for those injurious factors take effect first and foremost on the brain. In the course of the last decades changes have taken place in the political and social - and especially in the mercantile, industrial and agricultural - conditions of civilized nations which have brought about great changes in people's occupations, social position and property, and this at the cost of the nervous system, which is called upon to meet the increased social and economic demands by a greater expenditure of energy, often with quite inadequate opportunity for recuperation.'

The fault I have to find with these and many other similarly-worded opinions is not that they are mistaken but that they prove insufficient to explain the details in the picture of nervous disturbances and that they leave out of account precisely the most important of the aetiological factors involved. If we disregard the vaguer ways of being 'nervous' and consider the specific forms of nervous illness, we shall find that the injurious influence of civilization reduces itself in the main to the harmful suppression of the sexual life of civilized peoples (or classes) through the 'civilized' sexual morality prevalent in them.

I have tried to bring forward the evidence for this assertion in a number of technical papers.[1] I cannot repeat it here. I will, however, quote the most important of the arguments arising from my investigations.

Careful clinical observation allows us to distinguish two groups of nervous disorders: the *neuroses* proper and the *psychoneuroses*. In the former the disturbances (the symptoms), whether they show their effects in somatic or mental functioning, appear to be of a *toxic* nature. They behave exactly like the phenomena accompanying an excess or a deprivation of certain nerve poisons. These neuroses - which are commonly grouped together as 'neurasthenia' - can be induced by certain injurious influences in sexual life, without any hereditary taint being necessarily present; indeed, the form taken by the disease corresponds to the nature of these noxae, so that often enough the particular sexual aetiology can at once be deduced from the clinical picture. There is a total absence, on the other hand, of any such regular correspondence between the form of a nervous illness and the other injurious influences of civilization which are blamed by the authorities. We may, therefore, regard the sexual factor as the essential one in the causation of the neuroses proper.

[1] See my collection of short papers on the theory of the neuroses (1906).

With the psychoneuroses, the influence of heredity is more marked and the causation less transparent. A peculiar method of investigation known as psycho-analysis has, however, enabled us to recognize that the symptoms of these disorders (hysteria, obsessional neurosis, etc.) are *psychogenic* and depend upon the operation of unconscious (repressed) ideational complexes. This same method has also taught us what those unconscious complexes are and has shown that, quite generally speaking, they have a sexual content. They spring from the sexual needs of people who are unsatisfied and represent for them a kind of substitutive satisfaction. We must therefore view all factors which impair sexual life, suppress its activity or distort its aims as being pathogenic factors in the psychoneuroses as well.

The value of a theoretical distinction between toxic and psychogenic neuroses is, of course, not diminished by the fact that, in most people suffering from nervous illness, disturbances arising from both sources are to be observed.

The reader who is prepared to agree with me in looking for the aetiology of nervous illness pre-eminently in influences which damage sexual life, will also be ready to follow the further discussion, which is intended to set the theme of increasing nervous illness in a wider context.

Generally speaking, our civilization is built up on the suppression of instincts. Each individual has surrendered some part of his possessions - some part of the sense of omnipotence or of the aggressive or vindictive inclinations in his personality. From these contributions has grown civilization's common possession of material and ideal property. Besides the exigencies of life, no doubt it has been family feelings, derived from erotism, that have induced the separate individuals to make this renunciation. The renunciation has been a progressive one in the course of the evolution of civilization. The single steps in it were sanctioned by religion; the piece of instinctual satisfaction which each person had renounced was offered to the Deity as a sacrifice, and the communal property thus acquired was declared 'sacred'. The man who, in consequence of his unyielding constitution, cannot fall in with this suppression of instinct, becomes a 'criminal', an 'outlaw',[1] in the face of society - unless his social position or his exceptional capacities enable him to impose himself upon it as a great man, a 'hero'.

[1] [In English in the original]

The sexual instinct - or, more correctly, the sexual instincts, for analytic investigation teaches us that the sexual instinct is made up of many separate constituents or component instincts - is probably more strongly developed in man than in most of the higher animals; it is certainly more constant, since it has almost entirely overcome the periodicity to which it is tied in animals. It places extraordinarily large amounts of force at the disposal of civilized activity, and it does this in virtue of its especially marked characteristic of being able to displace its aim without materially diminishing in intensity. This capacity to exchange its originally sexual aim for another one, which is no longer sexual but which is psychically related to the first aim, is called the capacity for *sublimation*. In contrast to this displaceability, in which its value for civilization lies, the sexual instinct may also exhibit a particularly obstinate fixation which renders it unserviceable and which sometimes causes it to degenerate into what are described as abnormalities. The original strength of the sexual instinct probably varies in each individual; certainly the proportion of it which is suitable for sublimation varies. It seems to us that it is the innate constitution of each individual which decides in the first instance how large a part of his sexual instinct it will be possible to sublimate and make use of. In addition to this, the effects of experience and the intellectual influences upon his mental apparatus succeed in bringing about the sublimation of a further portion of it. To extend this process of displacement indefinitely is, however, certainly not possible, any more than is the case with the transformation of heat into mechanical energy in our machines. A certain amount of direct sexual satisfaction seems to be indispensable for most organizations, and a deficiency in this amount, which varies from individual to individual, is visited by phenomena which, on account of their detrimental effects on functioning and their subjective quality of unpleasure, must be regarded as an illness.

Further prospects are opened up when we take into consideration the fact that in man the sexual instinct does not originally serve the purposes of reproduction at all, but has as its aim the gaining of particular kinds of pleasure.[1] It manifests itself in this way in human infancy, during which it attains its aim of gaining pleasure not only from the genitals but from other parts of the body (the erotogenic zones), and can therefore disregard any objects other than these convenient ones. We call this stage the stage of *auto-erotism*, and the child's upbringing has, in our view, the task of restricting it, because to linger in it would make the sexual instinct uncontrollable and unserviceable later on. The development of the sexual instinct then proceeds from auto-erotism to object-love and from the autonomy of the erotogenic zones to their subordination under the primacy of the genitals, which are put at the service of reproduction.

13

During this development a part of the sexual excitation which is provided by the subject's own body is inhibited as being unserviceable for the reproductive function and in favourable cases is brought to sublimation. The forces that can be employed for cultural activities are thus to a great extent obtained through the suppression of what are known as the *perverse* elements of sexual excitation.

If this evolution of the sexual instinct is borne in mind, three stages of civilization can be distinguished: a first one, in which the sexual instinct may be freely exercised without regard to the aims of reproduction; a second, in which all of the sexual instinct is suppressed except what serves the aims of reproduction; and a third, in which only *legitimate* reproduction is allowed as a sexual aim. This third stage is reflected in our present-day 'civilized' sexual morality.

If we take the second of these stages as an average, we must point out that a number of people are, on account of their organization, not equal to meeting its demands. In whole classes of individuals the development of the sexual instinct, as we have described it above, from auto-erotism to object-love with its aim of uniting the genitals, has not been carried out correctly and sufficiently fully. As a result of these disturbances of development two kinds of harmful deviation from normal sexuality - that is, sexuality which is serviceable to civilization - come about; and the relation between these two is almost that of positive and negative.[1]

14

In the first place (disregarding people whose sexual instinct is altogether excessive and uninhibitable) there are the different varieties *perverts*, in whom an infantile fixation to a preliminary sexual aim has prevented the primacy of the reproductive function from being established, and the *homosexuals* or *inverts*, in whom, in a manner that is not yet quite understood, the sexual aim has been deflected away from the opposite sex. If the injurious effects of these two kinds of developmental disturbance are less than might be expected, this mitigation can be ascribed precisely to the complex way in which the sexual instinct is put together, which makes it possible for a person's sexual life to reach a serviceable final form even if one or more components of the instinct have been shut off from development. The constitution of people suffering from inversion - the homosexuals - is, indeed, often distinguished by their sexual instinct's possessing a special aptitude for cultural sublimation.

[1] Cf. my *Three Essays on the Theory of Sexuality* (1905d).

More pronounced forms of the perversions and of homosexuality, especially if they are exclusive, do, it is true, make those subject to them socially useless and unhappy, so that it must be recognized that the cultural requirements even of the second stage are a source of suffering for a certain proportion of mankind. The fate of these people who differ constitutionally from the rest varies, and depends on whether they have been born with a sexual instinct which by absolute standards is strong or comparatively weak. In the latter case - where the sexual instinct is in general weak - perverts succeed in totally suppressing the inclinations which bring them into conflict with the moral demands of their stage of civilization. But this, from the ideal point of view, is also the only thing they succeed in achieving; for, in order to effect this suppression of their sexual instinct, they use up the forces which they would otherwise employ in cultural activities. They are, as it were, inwardly inhibited and outwardly paralysed. What we shall be saying again later on about the abstinence demanded of men and women in the third stage of civilization applies to them too.

Where the sexual instinct is fairly intense, but perverse, there are two possible outcomes. The first, which we shall not discuss further, is that the person affected remains a pervert and has to put up with the consequences of his deviation from the standard of civilization. The second is far more interesting. It is that, under the influence of education and social demands, a suppression of the perverse instincts is indeed achieved, but it is a kind of suppression which is really no suppression at all. It can better be described as a suppression that has failed. The inhibited sexual instincts are, it is true, no longer expressed as such - and this constitutes the success of the process - but they find expression in other ways, which are quite as injurious to the subject and make him quite as useless for society as satisfaction of the suppressed instincts in an unmodified form would have done. This constitutes the failure of the process, which in the long run more than counterbalances its success. The substitutive phenomena which emerge in consequence of the suppression of the instinct amount to what we call nervous illness, or, more precisely, the psychoneuroses.[1] Neurotics are the class of people who, since they possess a recalcitrant organization, only succeed, under the influence of cultural requirements, in achieving a suppression of their instincts which is *apparent* and which becomes increasingly unsuccessful. They therefore only carry on their collaboration with cultural activities by a great expenditure of force and at the cost of an internal impoverishment, or are obliged at times to interrupt it and fall ill. I have described the neuroses as the 'negative' of the perversions because in the neuroses the perverse impulses, after being repressed, manifest themselves from the unconscious part of the mind - because the neuroses contain the same tendencies, though in a state of 'repression', as do the positive perversions.

[1] Cf. my introductory remarks above.

Experience teaches us that for most people there is a limit beyond which their constitution cannot comply with the demands of civilization. All who wish to be more noble-minded than their constitution allows fall victims to neurosis; they would have been more healthy if it could have been possible for them to be less good. The discovery that perversions and neuroses stand in the relation of positive and negative is often unmistakably confirmed by observations made on the members of one generation of a family. Quite frequently a brother is a sexual pervert, while his sister, who, being a woman, possesses a weaker sexual instinct, is a neurotic whose symptoms express the same inclinations as the perversions of her sexually more active brother. And correspondingly, in many families the men are healthy, but from a social point of view immoral to an undesirable degree, while the women are high-minded and over-refined, but severely neurotic.

It is one of the obvious social injustices that the standard of civilization should demand from everyone the same conduct of sexual life - conduct which can be followed without any difficulty by some people, thanks to their organization, but which imposes the heaviest psychical sacrifices on others; though, indeed, the injustice is as a rule wiped out by disobedience to the injunctions of morality.

These considerations have been based so far on the requirement laid down by the second of the stages of civilization which we have postulated, the requirement that every sexual activity of the kind described as perverse is prohibited, while what is called normal sexual intercourse is freely permitted. We have found that even when the line between sexual freedom and restriction is drawn at this point, a number of individuals are ruled out as perverts, and a number of others, who make efforts not to be perverts whilst constitutionally they should be so, are forced into nervous illness. It is easy to predict the result that will follow if sexual freedom is still further circumscribed and the requirements of civilization are raised to the level of the third stage, which bans all sexual activity outside legal marriage. The number of strong natures who openly oppose the demands of civilization will increase enormously, and so will the number of weaker ones who, faced with the conflict between the pressure of cultural influences and the resistance of their constitution, take flight into neurotic illness.

Let us now try to answer three questions that arise here:

(1) What is the task that is set to the individual by the requirements of the third stage of civilization?

(2) Can the legitimate sexual satisfaction that is permissible offer acceptable compensation for the renunciation of all other satisfactions?

(3) In what relation do the possible injurious effects of this renunciation stand to its exploitation in the cultural field?

The answer to the first question touches on a problem which has often been discussed and cannot be exhaustively treated here - that of sexual abstinence. Our third stage of civilization demands of individuals of both sexes that they shall practise abstinence until they are married and that all who do not contract a legal marriage shall remain abstinent throughout their lives. The position, agreeable to all the authorities, that sexual abstinence is not harmful and not difficult to maintain, has also been widely supported by the medical profession. It may be asserted, however, that the task of mastering such a powerful impulse as that of the sexual instinct by any other means than satisfying it is one which can call for the whole of a man's forces. Mastering it by sublimation, by deflecting the sexual instinctual forces away from their sexual aim to higher cultural aims, can be achieved by a minority and then only intermittently, and least easily during the period of ardent and vigorous youth. Most of the rest become neurotic or are harmed in one way or another. Experience shows that the majority of the people who make up our society are constitutionally unfit to face the task of abstinence. Those who would have fallen ill under milder sexual restrictions fall ill all the more readily and more severely before the demands of our cultural sexual morality of to-day; for we know no better safe-guard against the threat to normal sexual life offered by defective innate dispositions or disturbances of development than sexual satisfaction itself. The more a person is disposed to neurosis, the less can he tolerate abstinence; instincts which have been withdrawn from normal development, in the sense in which it has been described above, become at the same time all the more uninhibitable. But even those people who would have retained their health under the requirements of the second stage of civilization will now succumb to neurosis in great numbers. For the psychical value of sexual satisfaction increases with its frustration. The dammed-up libido is now put in a position to detect one or other of the weaker spots which are seldom absent in the structure of sexual life, and there to break through and obtain substitutive satisfaction of a neurotic kind in the form of pathological symptoms. Anyone who is able to penetrate the determinants of nervous illness will soon become convinced that its increase in our society arises from the intensification of sexual restrictions.

This brings us to the question whether sexual intercourse in legal marriage can offer full compensation for the restrictions imposed before marriage. There is such an abundance of material supporting a reply in the negative that we can give only the briefest summary of it. It must above all be borne in mind that our cultural sexual morality restricts sexual intercourse even in marriage itself, since it imposes on married couples the necessity of contenting themselves, as a rule, with a very few procreative acts. As a consequence of this consideration, satisfying sexual intercourse in marriage takes place only for a few years; and we must subtract from this, of course, the intervals of abstention necessitated by regard for the wife's health. After these three, four or five years, the marriage becomes a failure in so far as it has promised the satisfaction of sexual needs. For all the devices hitherto invented for preventing conception impair sexual enjoyment, hurt the fine susceptibilities of both partners and even actually cause illness. Fear of the consequences of sexual intercourse first brings the married couple's physical affection to an end; and then, as a remoter result, it usually puts a stop as well to the mental sympathy between them, which should have been the successor to their original passionate love. The spiritual disillusionment and bodily deprivation to which most marriages are thus doomed puts both partners back in the state they were in before their marriage, except for being the poorer by the loss of an illusion, and they must once more have recourse to their fortitude in mastering and deflecting their sexual instinct. We need not enquire how far men, by then in their maturer years, succeed in this task. Experience shows that they very frequently avail themselves of the degree of sexual freedom which is allowed them - although only with reluctance and under a veil of silence - by even the strictest sexual code. The 'double' sexual morality which is valid for men in our society is the plainest admission that society itself does not believe in the possibility of enforcing the precepts which it itself has laid down. But experience shows as well that women, who, as being the actual vehicle of the sexual interests of mankind, are only endowed in a small measure with the gift of sublimating their instincts, and who, though they may find a sufficient substitute for the sexual object in an infant at the breast, do not find one in a growing child - experience shows, I repeat, that women, when they are subjected to the disillusionments of marriage, fall ill of severe neuroses which permanently darken their lives.(Under the cultural conditions of to-day, marriage has long ceased to be a panacea for the nervous troubles of women; and if we doctors still advise marriage in such cases, we are nevertheless aware that, on the contrary, a girl must be very healthy if she is to be able to tolerate it, and we urgently advise our male patients not to marry any girl who has had nervous trouble before marriage. On the contrary, the cure for nervous illness arising from marriage would be marital unfaithfulness. But the more strictly a woman has been brought up and the more sternly she has submitted to the demands of civilization, the more she is afraid of taking this way out; and in the conflict between her desires and her sense of duty, she once more seeks refuge in a neurosis. Nothing protects her virtue as securely as an illness. Thus the married state, which is held out as a consolation to the sexual instinct of the civilized person in his youth, proves to be inadequate even to the demands of the actual period of life covered by it. There is no question of its being able to compensate for the deprivation which precedes it.

But even if the damage done by civilized sexual morality is admitted, it may be argued in reply to our third question that the cultural gain derived from such an extensive restriction of sexuality probably more than balances these sufferings, which, after all, only affect a minority in any severe form. I must confess that I am unable to balance gain against loss correctly on this point, but I could advance a great many more considerations on the side of the loss. Going back to the subject of abstinence, which I have already touched on, I must insist that it brings in its train other noxae besides those involved in the neuroses and that the importance of the neuroses has for the most part not been fully appreciated.

The retardation of sexual development and sexual activity at which our education and civilization aim is certainly not injurious to begin with. It is seen to be a necessity, when one considers the late age at which young people of the educated classes reach independence and are able to earn a living. (This reminds one, incidentally, of the intimate interconnection between all our cultural institutions and of the difficulty of altering any part of them without regard to the whole.) But abstinence continued long after the age of twenty is no longer unobjectionable for a young man; and it leads to other damage even when it does not lead to neurosis. People say, to be sure, that the struggle against such a powerful instinct, and the strengthening of all the ethical and aesthetic forces which are necessary for this struggle, 'steel' the character; and this is true for a few specially favourably organized natures. It must also be admitted that the differentiation of individual character, which is so marked in our day, has only become possible with the existence of sexual restriction. But in the vast majority of cases the struggle against sexuality eats up the energy available in a character and this at the very time when a young man is in need of all his forces in order to win his share and place in society. The relationship between the amount of sublimation possible and the amount of sexual activity necessary naturally varies very much from person to person and even from one calling to another. An abstinent artist is hardly conceivable; but an abstinent young *savant* is certainly no rarity. The latter can, by his self-restraint, liberate forces for his studies; while the former probably finds his artistic achievements powerfully stimulated by his sexual experience. In general I have not gained the impression that sexual abstinence helps to bring about energetic and self-reliant men of action or original thinkers or bold emancipators and reformers. Far more often it goes to produce well-behaved weaklings who later become lost in the great mass of people that tends to follow, unwillingly, the leads given by strong individuals.

The fact that the sexual instinct behaves in general in a self-willed and inflexible fashion is also seen in the results produced by efforts at abstinence. Civilized education may only attempt to suppress the instinct temporarily, till marriage, intending to give it free rein afterwards with the idea of then making use of it. But extreme measures are more successful against it than attempts at moderating it; thus the suppression often goes too far, with the unwished-for result that when the instinct is set free it turns out to be permanently impaired. For this reason complete abstinence in youth is often not the best preparation for marriage for a young man. Women sense this, and prefer among their suitors those who have already proved their masculinity with other women. The harmful results which the strict demand for abstinence before marriage produces in women's natures are quite especially apparent. It is clear that education is far from underestimating the task of suppressing a girl's sensuality till her marriage, for it makes use of the most drastic measures. Not only does it forbid sexual intercourse and set a high premium on the preservation of female chastity, but it also protects the young woman from temptation as she grows up, by keeping her ignorant of all the facts of the part she is to play and by not tolerating any impulse of love in her which cannot lead to marriage. The result is that when the girl's parental authorities suddenly allow her to fall in love, she is unequal to this psychical achievement and enters marriage uncertain of her own feelings. In consequence of this artificial retardation in her function of love, she has nothing but disappointments to offer the man who has saved up all his desire for her. In her mental feelings she is still attached to her parents, whose authority has brought about the suppression of her sexuality; and in her physical behaviour she shows herself frigid, which deprives the man of any high degree of sexual enjoyment. I do not know whether the anaesthetic type of woman exists apart from civilized education, though I consider it probable. But in any case such education actually breeds it, and these women who conceive without pleasure show little willingness afterwards to face the pains of frequent childbirth. In this way, the preparation for marriage frustrates the aims of marriage itself. When later on the retardation in the wife's development has been overcome and her capacity to love is awakened at the climax of her life as a woman, her relations to her husband have long since been ruined; and, as a reward for her previous docility, she is left with the choice between unappeased desire, unfaithfulness or a neurosis.

The sexual behaviour of a human being often *lays down the pattern* for all his other modes of reacting to life. If a man is energetic in winning the object of his love, we are confident that he will pursue his other aims with an equally unswerving energy; but if, for all sorts of reasons, he refrains from satisfying his strong sexual instincts, his behaviour will be conciliatory and resigned rather than vigorous in other spheres of life as well. A special application of this proposition that sexual life lays down the pattern for the exercise of other functions can easily be recognized in the female sex as a whole. Their upbringing forbids their concerning themselves intellectually with sexual problems though they nevertheless feel extremely curious about them, and frightens them by condemning such curiosity as unwomanly and a sign of a sinful disposition. In this way they are scared away from *any* form of thinking, and knowledge loses its value for them. The prohibition of thought extends beyond the sexual field, partly through unavoidable association, partly automatically, like the prohibition of thought about religion among men, or the prohibition of thought about loyalty among faithful subjects. I do not believe that women's 'physiological feeble-mindedness' is to be explained by a biological opposition between intellectual work and sexual activity, as Moebius has asserted in a work which has been widely disputed. I think that the undoubted intellectual inferiority of so many women can rather be traced back to the inhibition of thought necessitated by sexual suppression.

In considering the question of abstinence, the distinction is not nearly strictly enough made between two forms of it - namely abstention from any sexual activity whatever and abstention from sexual intercourse with the opposite sex. Many people who boast of succeeding in being abstinent have only been able to do so with the help of masturbation and similar satisfactions which are linked with the auto-erotic sexual activities of early childhood. But precisely because of this connection such substitutive means of sexual satisfaction are by no means harmless; they predispose to the numerous varieties of neuroses and psychoses which are conditional on an involution of sexual life to its infantile forms. Masturbation, moreover, is far from meeting the ideal demands of civilized sexual morality, and consequently drives young people into the same conflicts with the ideals of education which they hoped to escape by abstinence. Furthermore, it vitiates the character through *indulgence*, and this in more than one way. In the first place, it teaches people to achieve important aims without taking trouble and by easy paths instead of through an energetic exertion of force - that is, it follows the principle that *sexuality lays down the pattern* of behaviour; secondly, in the phantasies that accompany satisfaction the sexual object is raised to a degree of excellence which is not easily found again in reality. A witty writer (Karl Kraus in the Vienna paper *Die Fackel*) once expressed this truth in reverse by cynically remarking: 'Copulation is no more than an unsatisfying substitute for masturbation.'

The sternness of the demands of civilization and the difficulty of the task of abstinence have combined to make avoidance of the union of the genitals of the two opposite sexes into the central point of abstinence and to favour other kinds of sexual activity, which, it might be said, are equivalent to semi-obedience. Since normal intercourse has been so relentlessly persecuted by morality - and also, on account of the possibilities of infection, by hygiene - what are known as the perverse forms of intercourse between the two sexes, in which other parts of the body take over the role of the genitals, have undoubtedly increased in social importance.

These activities cannot, however, be regarded as being as harmless as analogous extensions in love-relationships. They are ethically objectionable, for they degrade the relationships of love between two human beings from a serious matter to a convenient game, attended by no risk and no spiritual participation. A further consequence of the aggravation of the difficulties of normal sexual life is to be found in the spread of homosexual satisfaction; in addition to all those who are homosexuals in virtue of their organization, or who became so in their childhood, there must be reckoned the great number of those in whom, in their maturer years, a blocking of the main stream of their libido has caused a widening in the side-channel of homosexuality.

All these unavoidable and unintended consequences of the requirement for abstinence converge in the one common result of completely ruining the preparation for marriage - marriage, which civilized sexual morality thinks should be the sole heir to the sexual impulses. Every man whose libido, as a result of masturbatory or perverse sexual practices, has become habituated to situations and conditions of satisfaction which are not normal, develops diminished potency in marriage. Women, too, who have been able to preserve their virginity with the help of similar measures, show themselves anaesthetic to normal intercourse in marriage. A marriage begun with a reduced capacity to love on both sides succumbs to the process of dissolution even more quickly than others. As a result of the man's weak potency, the woman is not satisfied, and she remains anaesthetic even in cases where her disposition to frigidity, derived from her education, could have been overcome by a powerful sexual experience. A couple like this finds more difficulties, too, in the prevention of children than a healthy one, since the husband's diminished potency tolerates the use of contraceptives badly. In this perplexity, sexual intercourse, as being the source of all their embarrassments, is soon given up, and with this the basis of married life is abandoned.

I ask any well-informed person to bear witness to the fact that I am not exaggerating but that I am describing a state of affairs of which equally bad instances can be observed over and over again. To the uninitiated it is hardly credible how seldom normal potency is to be found in a husband and how often a wife is frigid among married couples who live under the dominance of our civilized sexual morality, what a degree of renunciation, often on both sides, is entailed by marriage, and to what narrow limits married life - the happiness that is so ardently desired - is narrowed down. I have already explained that in these circumstances the most obvious outcome is nervous illness; but I must further point out the way in which a marriage of this kind continues to exercise its influence on the few children, or the only child born of it. At a first glance, it seems to be a case of transmission by inheritance; but closer inspection shows that it is really a question of the effect of powerful infantile impressions. A neurotic wife who is unsatisfied by her husband is, as a mother, over-tender and over-anxious towards her child, on to whom she transfers her need for love; and she awakens it to sexual precocity. The bad relations between its parents, moreover, excite its emotional life and cause it to feel love and hatred to an intense degree while it is still at a very tender age. Its strict upbringing, which tolerates no activity of the sexual life that has been aroused so early, lends support to the suppressing force and this conflict at such an age contains everything necessary for bringing about lifelong nervous illness.

I return now to my earlier assertion that, in judging the neuroses, their full importance is not as a rule taken into account. I do not mean by this the undervaluation of these states shown in their frivolous dismissal by relatives and in the boasting assurances by doctors that a few weeks of cold water treatment or a few months of rest and convalescence will cure the condition. These are merely the opinions of quite ignorant doctors and laymen and are mostly no more than words intended to give the sufferer a short-lived consolation. It is, on the contrary, a well-known fact that a chronic neurosis, even if it does not totally put an end to the subject's capacity for existence, represents a severe handicap in his life, of the same order, perhaps, as tuberculosis or a cardiac defect. The situation would even be tolerable if neurotic illness were to exclude from civilized activities only a number of individuals who were in any case of the weaker sort, and allowed the rest to play their part in it at the cost of troubles that were merely subjective. But, far from this being so, I must insist upon the view that neuroses, whatever their extent and wherever they occur, always succeed in frustrating the purposes of civilization, and in that way actually perform the work of the suppressed mental forces that are hostile to civilization. Thus, when society pays for obedience to its far-reaching regulations by an increase in nervous illness, it cannot claim to have purchased a gain at the price of sacrifices; it cannot claim a gain at all. Let us, for instance, consider the very common case of a woman who does not love her husband, because, owing to the conditions under which she entered marriage, she has no reason to love him, but who very much wants to love him, because that alone corresponds to the ideal of marriage to which she has been brought up. She will in that case suppress every impulse which would express the truth and contradict her endeavours to fulfil her ideal, and she will make special efforts to play the part of a loving, affectionate and attentive wife. The outcome of this self-suppression will be a neurotic illness; and this neurosis will in a short time have taken revenge on the unloved husband and have caused him just as much lack of satisfaction and worry as would have resulted from an acknowledgement of the true state of affairs. This example is completely typical of what a neurosis achieves. A similar failure to obtain compensation is to be seen after the suppression of impulses inimical to civilization which are not directly sexual. If a man, for example, has become over-kind as a result of a violent suppression of a constitutional inclination to harshness and cruelty, he often loses so much energy in doing this that he fails to carry out all that his compensatory impulses require, and he may, after all, do less good on the whole than he would have done without the suppression.

Let us add that a restriction of sexual activity in a community is quite generally accompanied by an increase of anxiety about life and of fear of death which interferes with the individual's capacity for enjoyment and does away with his readiness to face death for any purpose. A diminished inclination to beget children is the result, and the community or group of people in question is thus excluded from any share in the future. In view of this, we may well raise the question whether our 'civilized' sexual morality is worth the sacrifice which it imposes on us, especially if we are still so much enslaved to hedonism as to include among the aims of our cultural development a certain amount of satisfaction of individual happiness. It is certainly not a physician's business to come forward with proposals for reform; but it seemed to me that I might support the urgency of such proposals if I were to amplify Von Ehrenfels's description of the injurious effects of our 'civilized' sexual morality by pointing to the important bearing of that morality upon the spread of modern nervous illness.

www.ingramcontent.com/pod-product-compliance
Lightning Source LLC
Chambersburg PA
CBHW021605270326
41931CB00009B/1375